POLAR PLANET

Extreme Cold Environments

Chris Woodford

BROWN BEAR BOOKS

Published by Brown Bear Books Limited

An imprint of
The Brown Reference Group plc
68 Topstone Road
Redding
Connecticut
06896
USA
www.brownreference.com

Printed in China

9 8 7 6 5 4 3 2 1

For The Brown Reference Group plc
Project Editor: Ben Morgan
Deputy Editor: Dr. Rob Houston
Consultant: Professor Emeritus Robert
   G. White, Institute of Arctic Biology,
   University of Alaska Fairbanks
Designer: Reg Cox
Cartographers: Mark Walker
   and Darren Awuah
Picture Researcher: Clare Newman
Indexer: Kay Ollerenshaw
Design Manager: Lynne Ross
Managing Editor: Bridget Giles

Front cover: Polar bear, Arctic.
Inset (top): Inuit ice house, Arctic.
Inset (bottom): Walrus, Arctic.

Title page: Transantarctic Mountains, Antarctica.

The acknowledgments on p. 64 form part of this copyright page.

About this Book

The introductory pages of this book describe the biomes of the world and then the polar biomes. The five main chapters look at different aspects of the polar biomes: climate, plants, animals, people, and the future. Between the chapters are detailed maps that focus on key places within the biomes. The map pages are shown in the contents in italics, *like this*.

Throughout the book you'll also find boxed stories or fact files about the polar biomes. The icons here show what the boxes are about. At the end of the book is a glossary, which explains what all the difficult words mean. After the glossary is a list of books and websites for further research and an index, allowing you to find subjects anywhere in the book.

 Climate

 People

 Plants

 Future

 Animals

 Facts

Contents

Biomes of the World

Biologists divide the living world into major zones named biomes. Each biome has its own distinctive climate, plants, and animals.

Desert is the driest biome. There are hot deserts and cold ones.

Taiga is made up of conifer trees that can survive freezing winters.

If you were to walk all the way from the north of Canada to the Amazon rain forest, you'd notice the wilderness changing dramatically along the way.

Northern Canada is a freezing and barren place without trees, where only tiny brownish-green plants can survive in the icy ground. But trudge south for long enough and you enter a magical world of conifer forests, where moose, caribou, and wolves live. After several weeks, the conifers give out, and you reach the grass-covered prairies of the central United States. The farther south you go, the drier the land gets and the hotter the sun feels, until you find yourself hiking through a cactus-filled desert. But once you reach southern Mexico, the cacti start to disappear, and strange, tropical trees begin to take their place. Here, the muggy air is filled with the calls of exotic birds and the drone of tropical insects. Finally, in Colombia you cross the Andes mountain range—whose chilly peaks remind you a little of your starting point—and descend into the dense, swampy jungles of the Amazon rain forest.

Scientists have a special name for the different regions—such as desert, tropical rain forest, and prairie—that you'd pass through on such a journey. They call them biomes. Everywhere on Earth can be classified as being in one biome or another, and the same biome often appears in lots of

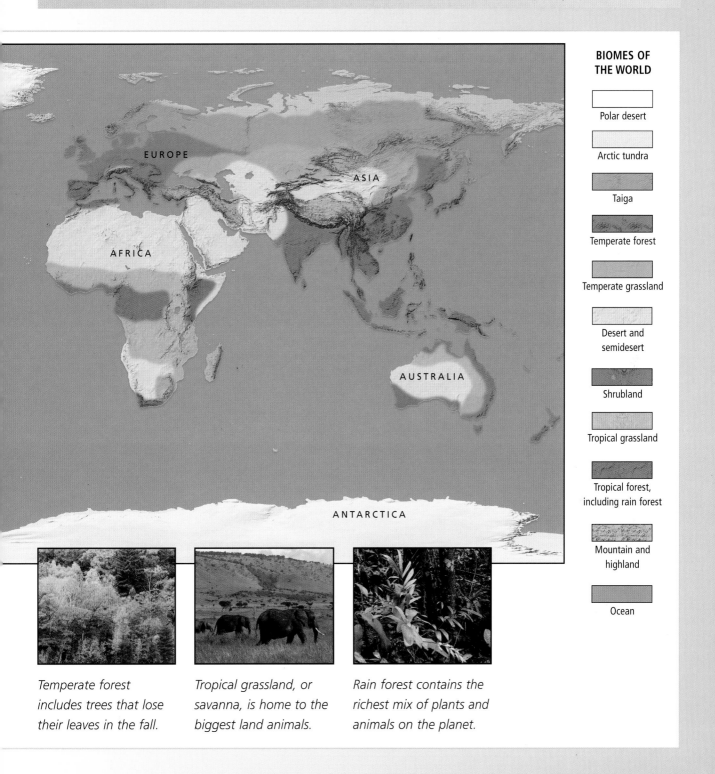

BIOMES OF THE WORLD

Polar desert

Arctic tundra

Taiga

Temperate forest

Temperate grassland

Desert and semidesert

Shrubland

Tropical grassland

Tropical forest, including rain forest

Mountain and highland

Ocean

EUROPE

ASIA

AFRICA

AUSTRALIA

ANTARCTICA

Temperate forest includes trees that lose their leaves in the fall.

Tropical grassland, or savanna, is home to the biggest land animals.

Rain forest contains the richest mix of plants and animals on the planet.

different places. For instance, there are areas of rain forest as far apart as Brazil, Africa, and Southeast Asia. Although the plants and animals that inhabit these forests are different, they live in similar ways. Likewise, the prairies of North America are part of the grassland biome, which also occurs in China, Australia, and Argentina. Wherever there are grasslands, there are grazing animals that feed on the grass, as well as large carnivores that hunt and kill the grazers.

The map on this page shows how the world's major biomes fit together to make up the biosphere—the zone of life on Earth.

The Polar Biomes

Next time you open your freezer, think what it would be like to live in an icy cold place. Perhaps you would need a layer of blubbery fat to keep you warm. Or maybe you would have a thick hairy coat and stand still for long periods.

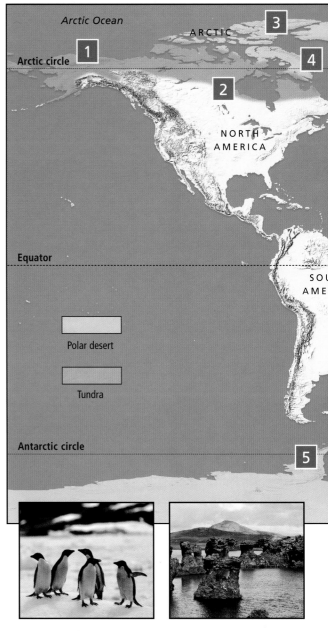

Polar desert

Tundra

The land of Antarctica is desert, but the seas are rich with wildlife.

Ice meets fire in Iceland, where volcanoes and hot springs warm the tundra.

Biting cold is only one of the problems of living near the poles. But it is the main reason that the Arctic (the region near the North Pole) and the Antarctic (the region near the South Pole) are such challenging places for animals and plants to survive in. The weather is coldest close to the poles, but milder farther away. Scientists therefore divide the polar regions into two different biomes: arctic tundra and polar desert.

Because the ground is frozen in the far north, trees cannot grow. Between the point where trees stop growing and the coast of the Arctic Ocean lies the tundra. It takes up about a tenth of Earth's surface and covers the northernmost parts of North America, Europe, and Asia. Wild, barren, and frozen solid in winter, the tundra bursts into life during summer in a swampy patchwork of colorful plants. Animals as different as the

musk ox and the arctic hare make this their home. Although there are many lakes and ponds formed from melting ice, much of the tundra gets as little rain as a desert.

Both the northern Arctic and the whole of Antarctica are too cold even for the hardy plants and animals of the tundra. The land

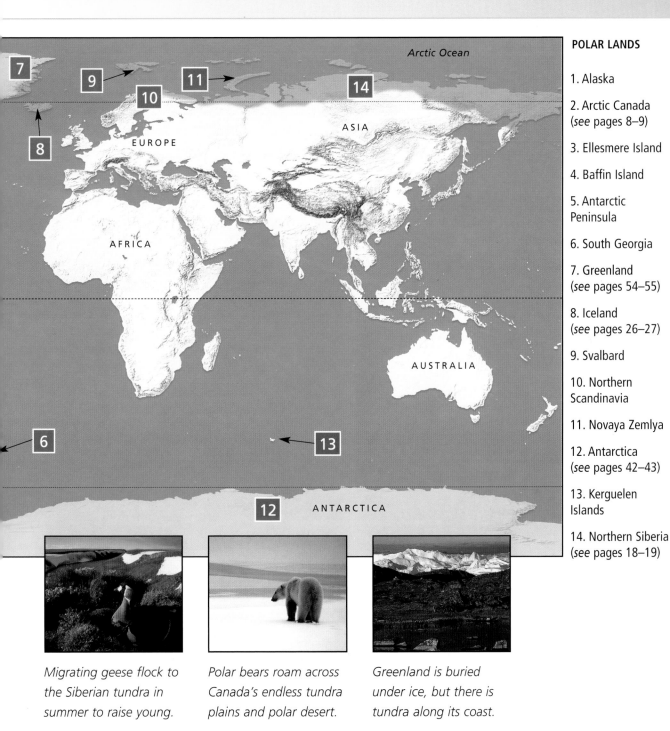

Migrating geese flock to the Siberian tundra in summer to raise young.

Polar bears roam across Canada's endless tundra plains and polar desert.

Greenland is buried under ice, but there is tundra along its coast.

there is either barren or covered with a permanent layer of ice that never thaws. There is even less rain or snow than in the tundra. As a result, this biome is known as polar desert. Very few plants and animals can survive year round in the polar desert. Seabirds nest there, but none are tough enough to survive entirely on land because there is not enough food. Most life in the polar desert is limited to the coast, where the animals can take food from the ocean. But even these areas are cold and harsh, with only short summers bringing relief from the dark and freezing winters.

North American Arctic

The tundra and polar deserts of Canada and Alaska are the emptiest parts of North America. The animals and people who live here have to endure long, dark, freezing winters, when temperatures can plunge to –58°F (–50°C).

 Fact File

▲ About 12,000 years ago, Canada was covered with ice and much of the United States was tundra. Tundra animals included mammoths, saber-toothed cats, lions, camels, and bison.

▲ The tundra is still home to some remarkable creatures, including musk oxen, lemmings, polar bears, and caribou.

▲ The United States bought Alaska from Russia in 1867 for just $7.2 million. That works out at roughly 2 cents an acre (or 5 cents a hectare). Today, Alaska's vast oil and mineral deposits make it worth many times as much.

Dall sheep live in the rugged mountains of Alaska, where Inupiat people hunt them by snowmobile.

GREENLAND

+ North magnetic pole

8 Ellesmere Island

6

Devon Island

9

Baffin Island

11

NORTH AMERICA · EUROPE · ASIA · AFRICA · SOUTH AMERICA · AUSTRALIA · ANTARCTICA

NUNAVUT

Iqaluit

Great Plain of the Koukdjuak

10

Atlantic Ocean

miles km
500
500
0 0

Hudson Bay

MANITOBA

Hudson Bay Lowlands

7

Lake Winnipeg

NEWFOUNDLAND

QUEBEC

St John's

ONTARIO

Winnipeg

PRINCE EDWARD ISLAND

N

Lake Superior

Quebec

NEW BRUNSWICK

NOVA SCOTIA

Montreal

1. Bering Strait
A narrow gap between Alaska and Siberia, about 40 miles (64 km) across.

2. Arctic National Wildlife Refuge
A protected area of Alaskan tundra that contains important breeding grounds for polar bears and caribou.

3. Brooks Range
A mountain range in Alaska. The highest point, Mount Chamberlain, is about a third the height of Mount Everest.

4. Great Bear Lake
A large freshwater lake—the largest entirely within Canada.

5. Arctic Ocean
The world's smallest ocean. During winter, most of the Arctic is covered with sea ice.

6. North Magnetic Pole
The place to which compasses point. The magnetic pole is about 1,000 miles (1,600 km) from the North Pole. It changes location slowly over the years.

7. Hudson Bay Lowlands
A vast area of swampy tundra and wetlands.

8. Ellesmere Island
Cape Columbia, at the top of the island, is the northernmost part of North America.

9. Devon Island
Parts of this rocky desert island look just like Mars. NASA uses the island to test Martian probes and buggies.

10. Great Plain of the Koukdjuak
A wetland area with many rivers, ponds, and streams.

11. Baffin Island
Baffin Island is the world's fifth largest island. No trees grow there, but there are many lakes. The east coast contains high mountain peaks.

Across the Bering Bridge

Between Alaska and Siberia is a narrow passage of water called the Bering Strait, but this has not always been there. During Earth's ice ages, the sea level fell as water turned to ice. As a result, the land between Alaska and Siberia emerged above sea level, forming a land bridge.

The land bridge across the Bering Strait allowed animals to walk across. Ancient species of horses and camels wandered west from Alaska to Asia and evolved into the zebras and camels we know today. Some animals moved east, including caribou (below), lemmings, foxes, and wolves. The Native Americans, who were the first people to settle in North America, also probably crossed the Bering bridge.

Polar Climate

The pattern of weather that occurs in one region during a typical year is called the region's climate. In the Arctic and the Antarctic, the climate is very cold and dry, and this is why the polar biomes exist.

Have you ever stopped to wonder why there is snow and ice around the polar regions at the top and bottom of our planet, but not around the middle, where there are savannas (tropical grasslands) and tropical forests instead? The answer lies in the way Earth moves as it travels through space.

Earth travels around the sun in a giant circle called an orbit, taking a year to complete one orbit. Besides orbiting the sun, our planet is continually spinning around, making one whole turn each day. It stays roughly upright as it spins, with the poles at the top and bottom. Because the poles never face the sun directly, the sunlight they receive is spread over a wide area, and this is why the poles are so cold. You'd notice the weak sunlight if you stood on the North Pole in the middle of a sunny day. Even in midsummer the sun would be very low in the sky, and its rays would hardly warm your skin.

Right: This photo shows the sun in several different positions during its path across the sky on a midsummer night in Antarctica. The middle two images of the sun were produced around midnight. On this night, for viewers on the antarctic circle, the sun does not set at all, but dips toward the horizon. The sun then continues its wide circle around the sky.

The temperature in Antarctica rarely rises above freezing, even in midsummer. There is hardly any liquid freshwater for plants to absorb.

The Midnight Sun

A strange thing about the polar regions is their unusual pattern of daylight. There is only one day and one night each year at the North and South Poles, each lasting six months. The sun stays just above the horizon for six months of the year, circling through the sky once every 24 hours. It gradually sinks lower, until it disappears altogether for the next six months. Once the sun has set, the pole is plunged into darkness for half a year, and the weather turns bitterly cold.

At the North Pole, the permanently dark winter lasts from September 21 to March 21, with midwinter on December 21. The opposite happens at the South Pole, where it is summer from September to March.

The strange days and seasons happen because the poles lie at the ends of Earth's axis—the imaginary line around which our planet spins. While the rest of the planet spins around, turning through day and night every 24 hours, the poles stay in the same place, a bit like the ends of a spinning top. Because Earth's axis is slightly tilted, the poles take turns facing the sun or facing away, and this is why they spend six months in sunlight followed by six months in darkness.

Arctic Circle

As you travel from the North Pole, the pattern of light and darkness becomes more normal. Once you reach the arctic circle—an imaginary circle drawn a certain distance around the North Pole—there is only one day each year when the sun does not rise at all, and only one day when it does not set. The same happens at the antarctic circle.

Six months of continuous daylight might seem like enough to make the poles positively tropical places, but there are some complications. Not only is the sun low in the sky, but the ice and snow at the poles reflect away most of the sunlight. As a result, most of the sun's heat bounces straight back into space, and this makes the poles even more chilly than they would otherwise be.

Poles Apart

Many people think the Arctic and Antarctic are much the same, except for being on opposite ends of the world. But there are important differences. For one thing, the Arctic is mostly ocean below its layer of snow and ice, while a huge continent makes up most of the Antarctic. Although the surface of the Arctic Ocean is frozen, the water

Dark blue indicates high rainfall in these world maps. The polar regions, like desert regions elsewhere,

are very pale blue in both the January and July maps because they receive so little rain throughout the year.

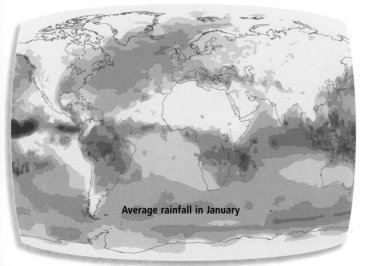

Average rainfall in January

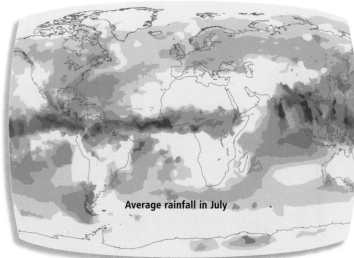

Average rainfall in July

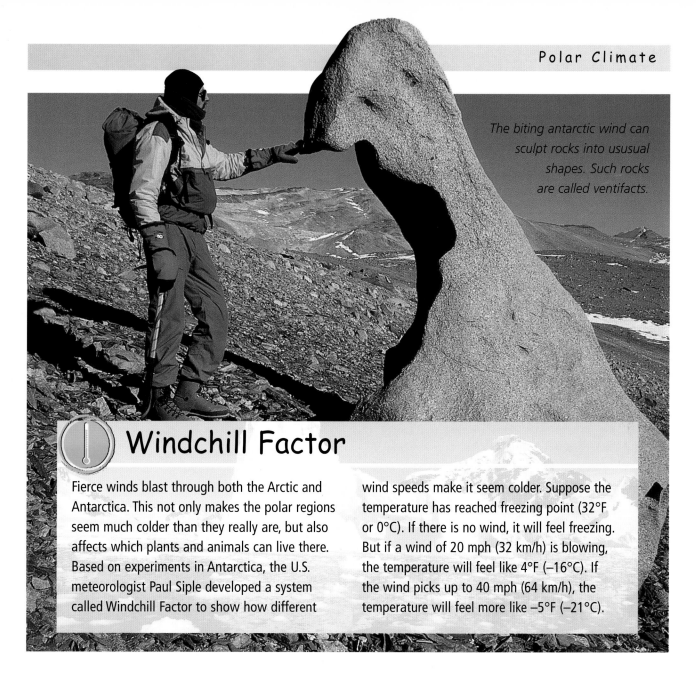

The biting antarctic wind can sculpt rocks into ususual shapes. Such rocks are called ventifacts.

(!) Windchill Factor

Fierce winds blast through both the Arctic and Antarctica. This not only makes the polar regions seem much colder than they really are, but also affects which plants and animals can live there. Based on experiments in Antarctica, the U.S. meteorologist Paul Siple developed a system called Windchill Factor to show how different wind speeds make it seem colder. Suppose the temperature has reached freezing point (32°F or 0°C). If there is no wind, it will feel freezing. But if a wind of 20 mph (32 km/h) is blowing, the temperature will feel like 4°F (−16°C). If the wind picks up to 40 mph (64 km/h), the temperature will feel more like −5°F (−21°C).

Red or orange areas of these maps are hot regions with high temperatures. Blue indicates low temperatures.

The antarctic region is cold in both July and January, but the Arctic warms to higher temperatures in July.

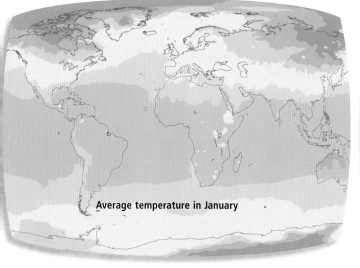

Average temperature in January

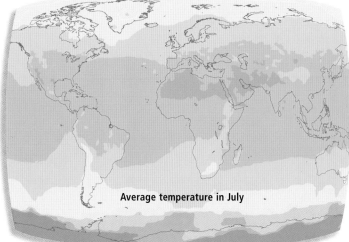

Average temperature in July

below keeps moving. A warm ocean current from the Atlantic keeps the Arctic warmer in winter than it would otherwise be. The surface ice moves and sometimes splits, producing large stretches of open water. Nearby landmasses, such as Alaska and Siberia, also provide some heat. Antarctica, however, is cut off from warm waters by a cold ocean current that flows around the continent. It is also very far from other landmasses, and its surface is much higher than sea level, which makes it even colder.

Average winter temperatures in the Arctic vary greatly across the region, but typically reach lows of about –30°F (–34°C). The average temperature in the arctic summer is about 50°F (10°C). That is warm enough to thaw the frozen surface in the tundra region, allowing it to burst into life in the brief arctic summer.

The Arctic is warmer than most people believe. In the early 1990s, a Russian icebreaker forced its way through sea ice to the North Pole with a party of tourists on

Climographs

Each place in the world has its own pattern of weather. The typical pattern of weather that happens in one place during a year is called climate. It is possible to show a place's climate on a climograph, such as the one shown here for St. Louis. The letters along the bottom are the months of the year. The numbers on the left and the small bars show rainfall, and the numbers on the right and the curved line show temperature. You can see at a glance that St. Louis is hottest in July, but December is the driest month.

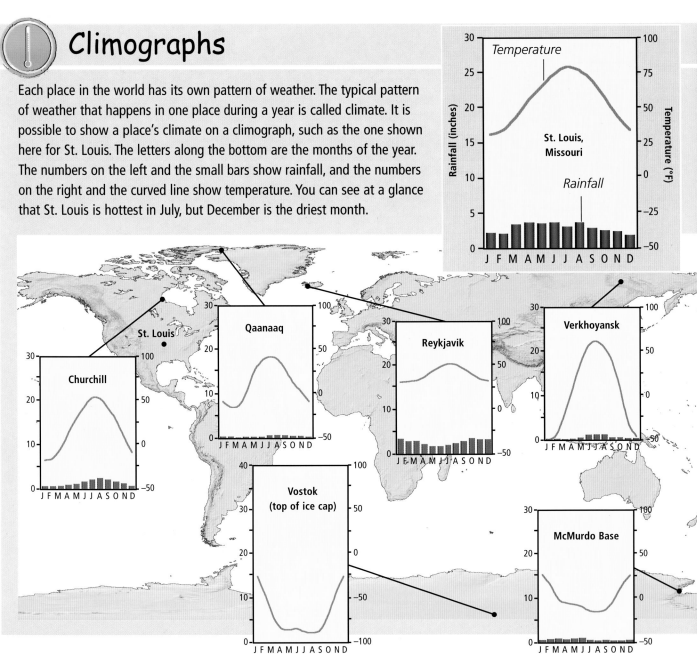

Antarctica is so dry that some parts, including the Dry Valleys, are free of ice. Visitors remark how the Dry Valleys seem like the surface of Mars. When NASA was testing vehicles for durability for its Viking *mission to Mars in the 1970s, it brought them to the Dry Valleys.*

board. They held a barbecue at the pole, and some of them even went for a chilly swim! Swimming in the Antarctic Ocean is another matter. There, the average winter temperature is –15°F (–26°C), and the average summer temperature is only 26°F (–3°C). High on top of the antarctic ice cap, the conditions are even more extreme: summer temperatures of –26°F (–32°C) drop to an average of –76°F (–60°C) in winter. In other words, summer on the antarctic ice cap is often colder even than an arctic winter. It is no place for a summer barbecue. If you made a hole in the antarctic ice and hauled out a small fish, it would freeze solid in minutes.

Water, Water, Everywhere?

Although there are masses of ice and snow at the poles, the Arctic and Antarctica are among the driest places on Earth. The South Pole receives only a small amount of snow (about 2 inches or 50 mm) each year. Some parts of Antarctica receive less than a tenth of the rainfall or snow of a typical desert. The Dry Valleys of the Transantarctic Mountains are drier than the Sahara.

The Arid Poles

The arid polar climate is caused by cold air sinking over the poles. The air in Earth's atmosphere is continually moving, rising in certain places and sinking in others. When air rises it cools down, and this makes moisture in the air turn to rain or snow, which fall back to Earth. Sinking air comes from high in the atmosphere, so it has already lost its moisture and become dry. As it hits the ground, it spreads outward and stops moister air from moving in. The world's largest deserts and the poles lie in areas where dry air is continually sinking, resulting in clear blue skies and very dry weather.

The Arctic is wetter than Antarctica, though it is still very dry. It typically gets about 8 inches (200 mm) of rain and snow each year, and the tundra tends to retain the water that falls there. There are two reasons for this: underneath the tundra is a layer of permanently frozen soil called permafrost through which water cannot seep away; and above the tundra is a layer of cold air. Cold air makes it difficult for water on the ground to evaporate (turn to vapor), because air can hold very little moisture when it is cold. Together, the permafrost and the cold air keep water sandwiched inside the tundra. In summer, the water trickles across the flat tundra landscape in small streams and rivers, or it collects in ponds, lakes, and marshes.

Alpine Cold

The same cold conditions that create tundra landscapes in the Arctic also happen on high mountains elsewhere on Earth. A lot of plants that grow in the Arctic also grow on mountains. Tundra stretches into the Rockies far to the south of the Arctic. The conditions are not the same, though. Outside the Arctic, it is often far wetter, and the strange sequence of very dark winters and bright summers does not exist. The biome on top of high mountains is called alpine tundra. Unlike arctic tundra, alpine tundra does not have a permafrost layer (see box).

The Polar Seasons

If you visited the arctic tundra in summer and winter, you might think you had gone to two completely different places. In summer, when daylight lasts nearly 24 hours, the tundra is a mixture of green, treeless plains, swamps, bogs, and lakes. In some places

Permafrost

If you dig a hole in your garden, you'll probably find nothing but damp brown soil. Try to do the same thing in the tundra, however, and your spade will suddenly scrape against a thick layer of permanently frozen soil: permafrost. Permafrost is so named because it is permanently frosty, even in the middle of summer. It is usually about 20 inches (50 cm) below the tundra's surface, though in winter the top layer of soil is frozen, too.

Permafrost plays an important part in the tundra's ecology. It stops water from draining away, and so keeps the tundra wet and marshy in summer, like the tundra on Banks Island, Canada (below). Scientists are worried that climate change is now making permafrost melt in Siberia and other parts of the Arctic, which could harm the tundra.

there is more water than land, and traveling can be difficult. For about two months in summer, the tundra comes alive with wildlife: Insects such as mosquitoes and flies, wetland birds and fish, roaming grizzly bears, and swooping owls and jaegers are to be found. In winter, the Arctic is another world entirely. The tundra freezes solid, and ice covers the lakes, rivers, and sea. Plants vanish beneath the blanket of ice, and most of the animals head south for winter. The nights grow so long that they seem to merge together, and blinding snowstorms can make it almost impossible to see.

If the summer thaw is short in the Arctic, it is almost nonexistent in Antarctica. Much of the sea ice around the continent melts, but the land stays frozen solid. Only the coast can support seabirds and other animals briefly in summer, but most of these soon move northward away from Antarctica before the long winter sets in.

Aurorae (the northern and southern lights) dance around the sky in the polar regions. They are caused by particles from the sun hitting Earth's atmosphere.

Siberian Tundra

A vast belt of tundra stretches across north Siberia in Russia, from the northern edge of the taiga to the coast of the Arctic Ocean. The Siberian tundra comes to life each year after the spring thaw. Countless ponds and lakes form from meltwater, and the ground turns into a carpet of mosses, lichens, and flowering shrubs.

SWEDEN
NORWAY
Arctic
FINLAND
Murmansk •
Barents Sea
Novaya Zemlya
2
Archangel •
Yam.
Peninsu
1
Ural Mountains
Ob River
R U S S I A N

NORTH AMERICA
EUROPE
ASIA
AFRICA
SOUTH AMERICA
AUSTRALIA
ANTARCTICA
KAZAKSTAN

Tundra in Trouble

One of the biggest threats to Siberia's tundra comes from oil and gas extraction. In the past, wells took up vast areas. Vehicles and machinery crushed the fragile tundra plants, and caused the permafrost (frozen soil) to thaw earlier and collapse. It takes decades for the thin layer of soil to form again. People can now use modern techniques that are less destructive, but the tundra habitat may still suffer in less obvious ways.

Scientists are worried that melting permafrost will increase the flow of rivers into the Arctic Ocean. The extra water would make the ocean less salty and could damage the habitats of many species. The melting could also cause the low-lying arctic tundra to sink into the sea.

Map labels:

nz-Josef Land

N

O c e a n

Franz-Josef Land · Severnaya Zemlya · New Siberian Islands · Wrangel Island · Chuckchi Sea · Chukchi Peninsula · Aleutian Islands (U.S.) · Bering Strait

[7] Wrangel Island · [8]

Yttygren Island

Kara Sea · [6] · East Siberian Sea · Chukchi Autonomous Region · Bering Sea

Laptev Sea

Taymyr Peninsula · Pacific Ocean

[5]
• Dickson

North Siberian Lowland

• Norilsk

Kolyma River

Kamchatka Peninsula

[4]

Yenisey River

Verkhoyansk Mountains · Lena River · • Verkhoyansk

• Oimyakon · • Magadan

F E D E R A T I O N

• Yakutsk

Petropavlovsk-Kamchatskiy •

Central Siberian Plateau

Sea of Okhotsk

S i b e r i a

miles · km
300

Tomsk
• Kemerovo
osibirsk
Barnaul · • Krasnoyarsk

Sakhalin

300

0 — 0

---

1. Ural Mountains
This long mountain range separates Europe from Asia.

2. Novaya Zemlya
Much of this island is covered permanently in ice, but low-lying, ice-free areas are tundra. Wildlife includes polar bears, walruses, and lemmings.

3. Yamal Peninsula
Developers have quickly moved into this region to extract oil. The land is so low-lying that it will sink into the ocean if environmental damage melts the permafrost.

4. Yenisey River
This immense river is often frozen from November through May.

5. Dickson
This small port on the Arctic coast is one of the most northerly towns in Russia. The winters are long and dark. The people there depend on fishing, hunting, and reindeer farming.

6. Severnaya Zemlya
A group of barren islands, unknown until explorers discovered it in 1913.

7. Wrangel Island
An island where seals and polar bears breed.

8. Whalebone Alley
On Yttygren Island, this important archaeological site is an ancient Eskimo monument made from the skulls of 60 bowhead whales.

Siberia Facts

▲ In the southeastern Siberian tundra lies the town of Oimyakon, where a temperature of −94°F (−70°C) was recorded. When it is that cold, your breath freezes and tinkles to the ground with a noise the locals call "the whispering of the stars."

▲ The Siberian tundra is so cold that plants grow extremely slowly. Mosses grow about as much in a year as your fingernails grow in a week.

▲ The Siberian tundra belt is about 300 miles (482 km) wide, which is about as far as the distance between St. Louis and Chicago.

Polar Plants

Plants need sunlight and water, as well as soft ground for their roots. But the land near the poles is frozen solid and dark for months on end—and it can be drier than the Sahara. Only the world's toughest plants can survive in this extreme environment.

Imagine what it would be like to live in Greenland. You would need plenty of thick clothes to help keep you warm, including boots and gloves to keep your feet and hands from freezing. In winter, you might want a flashlight for those days when the sun never seems to rise, and in summer, you would need sunglasses to protect your eyes from the dazzling snow and ice.

People can adapt to life in difficult places, but only if they remember to pack the right equipment. Likewise, but over millions of years, plants can adapt to live in the freezing Arctic and Antarctic, but they have to be pretty remarkable plants to survive.

The biggest threats to a polar plant are the numbing cold, the darkness, the icy winds, and the lack of sheltered places in which to

Red bearberry leaves brighten this view of tundra plant life in the Yukon Territory, Canada. Like arctic tundra elsewhere, the Yukon tundra has no trees.

Sun Watchers

Although summer days are long in the tundra, sunlight is weak because the sun stays low in the sky. To make the most of the weak light, some plants turn around to track the sun through the sky. The butter-yellow flowers (right) of the arctic poppy look like satellite dishes as they turn to follow the sun. Just as a satellite dish gathers radio waves and focuses them on an antenna at the center, so the petals of the arctic poppy focus warmth onto the center of the flower, helping the seeds grow quickly. Other plants, such as arctic avens, use this trick, too.

grow. But polar plants have overcome all of these problems. Just as you would wrap yourself in a sweater to keep warm, so are the stems and leaves of many arctic plants covered in little furry hairs. Sweaters keep us warm by trapping a layer of air next to our bodies. In the same way, the hairs of arctic plants trap warmer air around them. One arctic plant has such a thick woolly coat that it is named the woolly lousewort.

Plants use sunlight to grow through a process called photosynthesis. They trap the energy in light and use it to combine water and carbon dioxide (a gas in the air) to make food. Because the poles are dark throughout winter, plants cannot grow. So they either stay inactive under the ice or die after setting seed, and the seeds wait for the next summer. Tundra plants grow quickly in

the short summer, making good use of the long days to flower and produce seeds as soon as possible before winter begins again. Many tundra plants don't even bother to flower—instead they grow sideways and split into new individuals, making clones of themselves.

Cold and darkness are not the only problems facing polar plants. There are also gale-force winds and freezing blizzards that would kill many ordinary plants in minutes. For this reason, most polar

Rather than standing tall against the gales, the little arctic dwarf willow grows along the ground. A coat of downy hairs protects it from the cold.

Why No Trees?

One definition of the polar biomes is that they are places where no trees grow. Trees flourish in the taiga biome to the south of the Arctic, but the tundra and polar deserts are treeless. Why? The most obvious answer is that it is too cold. Yet this cannot be the whole explanation, because the spruce trees that grow along the northern edge of the taiga can survive winter temperatures that are even colder than those on the arctic coast.

The main reason that trees do not grow is the permafrost, the permanently frozen ground underneath the surface layers of the thin tundra soil. The permafrost makes it impossible for roots to grow any deeper than a few inches. Another problem is the lack of shelter from the freezing wind, which stunts growth. And in the polar deserts, there simply isn't enough water for large plants.

in Greenland alone. Conditions are different in Antarctica, though, where only two species of flowering plants exist (see page 25).

Of the plants that provide food for the creatures of the Arctic, none are more important than those with berries. Although grizzly bears and polar bears are mainly meat eaters, they are sometimes forced to be vegetarian when prey is in short supply. One of their favorite snacks is the aptly named bearberry. The seeds in bearberries pass through the bear unharmed and sprout if they fall on good ground.

plants tend to grow very near the ground, where the wind is slower and the temperature slightly warmer. Willows grow as shrubs or trees in warmer parts of the world. In the Arctic, the twisted stems of dwarf willows snake across the ground, growing sideways instead of upward. Rarely more than a few inches tall, they escape the worst of the wind and the ice in this way.

Some arctic plants turn the wind to their advantage, using it to help them spread their seeds farther and increase their chances of survival. One of the best-known arctic plants, cotton grass, has fluffy heads at the top of its thin stems. The heads produce thousands of very small seeds, which are caught by the wind. They swirl into the air and fly far away to grow in new places.

Despite the cruel conditions, as many as 1,000 species of plants thrive in the arctic region, and 40 different flowering plants grow

In the Polar Garden

Gardeners around the world often divide their plots into different areas, such as rock gardens, rose gardens, and wildflower meadows. This may seem an original idea, but it is only a copy of what nature does by itself. In the tundra, for example, plants form different types of gardens depending on how much water is available. In marshy areas, mosses form a layer under other plants, such as grasslike plants called sedges. In less soggy places, small shrubs are common. They burst with berries in summer and turn orange or red

Above: The seed heads of cotton grass are a common sight in the tundra in August. Inuit people use the silky white "cotton" to stuff pillows and mattresses.

Left: In late summer, bears and other tundra creatures feed on tough black crowberries. People also use these berries to make pies, soups, and jellies.

The Tropical Antarctic

The world's coldest continent is one of the best places to find evidence of past eras, because samples are preserved by the cold and undisturbed by human activity. Even a footprint in the moss of Antarctica can last for decades. Paleontologists (scientists who study fossils) have found many remains in Antarctica, including dinosaurs and a huge armadillo the size of a Volkswagen Beetle.

Such animals could have lived in Antarctica only if the continent once had much more plant life than it does today. Scientists think Antarctica was joined to Africa, India, and Australia about 100 million years ago. Together they formed a vast continent—Gondwana—that was north of the equator and had a tropical climate. Fossils of tropical plants remain in Antarctica to this day, hidden under the ice.

in the fall. Wildflowers, such as arctic poppies, tend to grow in the rocky parts of the tundra where it is very dry. The rocks themselves may be covered in lichens and mosses—the true survivors of the polar world.

Polar Survivors

Plants do grow in the polar desert of Antarctica, but they are very different from the wildflowers and berries that grow on the tundra. Although life in Antarctica is at its most extreme, algae, lichens, and mosses still manage to survive.

By definition, algae are not plants. They are simpler, plantlike organisms that live by photosynthesis, but have no true leaves, stems, or roots. In some places, the rocks and ice of Antarctica are turned brilliant red, yellow, or green by patches of algae living on the surface.

A lichen is a slightly more sophisticated form of life, made up of a fungus and an alga living together. Lichens are among the hardiest living things on Earth. They can grow on bare rock, and in laboratories they can survive temperatures almost as low as absolute zero (–273°C or –460°F)—the lowest temperature possible. Lichens grow in both Antarctica and the Arctic, coloring almost

Hidden Life

Two antarctic lakes are thought to contain very different kinds of life. Lake Vanda in the Dry Valleys is permanently frozen over with ice about as thick as the length of a small car. Yet sunlight seeps through, warming the water beneath to a balmy 77°F (25°C)—the temperature of a tropical ocean. In this indoor antarctic swimming pool, a variety of algae, bacteria, and other microorganisms lead a cozy life.

Lake Vostok is about the same size as Lake Ontario but twice as deep. It is also possibly the world's most remarkable lake, because it is buried under about 2 miles (4 km) of ice. Because it has been cut off from the rest of the world for millions of years, scientists believe it could contain extraordinary new species—or perhaps none at all. Scientists are trying to figure out how to explore the lake with robots, in a way that will not contaminate it and kill off any life that may be there.

any surface, from rocks to decayed bones, with blotches of orange and gold. They are especially common on darker rocks, which warm up in sunlight more than pale rocks. Lichens provide the starting point for another type of polar survivor: the mosses.

Reindeer moss is not a moss but a type of lichen, eaten by reindeer. This picture also shows red leaves of a bearberry bush poking through the lichen.

Tundra Plants of North America

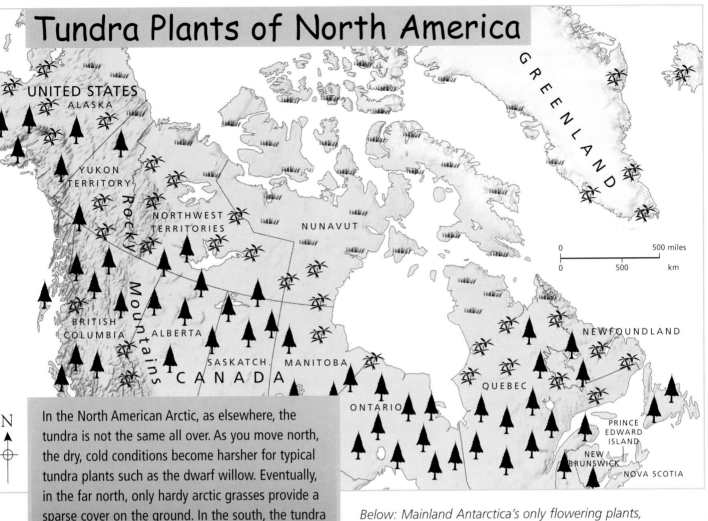

GREENLAND

UNITED STATES
ALASKA

YUKON TERRITORY

Rocky Mountains

NORTHWEST TERRITORIES

NUNAVUT

BRITISH COLUMBIA

ALBERTA

SASKATCH. MANITOBA

CANADA

ONTARIO

QUEBEC

NEWFOUNDLAND

PRINCE EDWARD ISLAND

NEW BRUNSWICK

NOVA SCOTIA

0   500 miles
0   500   km

N

In the North American Arctic, as elsewhere, the tundra is not the same all over. As you move north, the dry, cold conditions become harsher for typical tundra plants such as the dwarf willow. Eventually, in the far north, only hardy arctic grasses provide a sparse cover on the ground. In the south, the tundra plants are mixed with the conifer forests of the taiga for many miles. Tundra plants also live much farther south on the high ground of the Rockies.

Conifer trees form the forests of the taiga.

Dwarf willow is a shrub that can grow in tundra but not in polar desert.

Hardy arctic grasses sparsely cover the ground in dry tundra and polar desert.

Below: Mainland Antarctica's only flowering plants, antarctic hairgrass (upper plant) and pearlwort (lower plant) shelter in a moss-lined rock crevice.

By coating rocks with a rough surface, lichens give mosses a foothold in which to grow. Crevices in the moss and lichen trap windblown dirt, forming a thin layer of soil. This soil provides anchorage and nutrients for Antarctica's only two flowering plant species: antarctic hairgrass and pearlwort (colobanthus). Both live only in the Antarctic Peninsula, where the climate is milder than in the continent's interior.

Iceland

Iceland is a striking mixture of hot and cold, famous for huge glaciers, active volcanoes, and geysers. A warm ocean current makes the island warmer than most Arctic lands, but the plant life is mainly tundra.

The Vatna Glacier is an ice cap covering the highlands of southern Iceland. It gives birth to glaciers that flow to the lowlands, where they melt, forming rivers.

Iceland Facts

▲ Only one mammal, the arctic fox, lived on Iceland before people arrived. People introduced reindeer and other animals for farming and transportation. Rats, mice, and mink were carried to the island accidentally on ships.

▲ There are more than 200 volcanoes on Iceland, many of them still active.

▲ Vatna Glacier is as large in area as all the other glaciers of Europe combined.

▲ All the world's geysers are named after a gigantic spring called Great Geysir in southwestern Iceland. It shoots a jet of boiling water 200 feet (60 m) into the air.

1. Reykjavik
The capital of Iceland.

2. Westfjords
This mountainous region is a stronghold of Iceland's largest bird, the rare white-tailed eagle, also called the gray sea eagle.

3. Heimaey
Tiny island off the south coast, with its own active volcano.

4. Great Geysir
The country's most spectacular geyser.

5. Mount Hekla
A large volcano that has erupted many times, most recently in 1970.

6. Desert
Since people settled in Iceland in the year 875, farm animals have overgrazed the fragile tundra plant life. Now, areas of central Iceland are barren desert, even though Iceland's climate is moist.

7. Mount Hvannadals
At 6,952 feet (2,119 m), this is Iceland's highest mountain.

8. Lake Myvatn
Teeming with ducks and other birdlife, this lake is considered one of the natural wonders of the world.

9. Vatna Glacier
A huge glacier in southeast Iceland.

The World's Biggest Duck Pond

It is easy to see why Lake Myvatn is one of Iceland's biggest tourist attractions. Not only is it stunningly beautiful, it is also home to more species of duck (15 in all) than any other lake in the world. Around the lake are volcanic craters, bubbling mud pools, hot springs, and other signs of volcanic activity. Algae flourish in the lake's mineral-rich water, providing food for crabs and midges, and these in turn feed fish and birds. Lake Myvatn means "Lake Midge." Although the swarms of midges are unpopular with the tourists, they are one of the reasons why wildlife flourishes there.

Polar Animals

Did you know that the hair on a polar bear can carry sunlight, like tiny fiber-optic cables? Or that seagulls keep their legs much colder than their body to avoid losing heat? These are just two of the ingenious ways in which animals survive the hardships of life at the poles.

The different climates of the arctic and antarctic regions mean very different types of plants grow in each place. Likewise, the animals living near the north and south poles are also different. In the arctic tundra there are lots of land mammals, including grizzly bears, foxes, caribou, musk oxen, and lemmings. In Antarctica, however, there are no native land mammals. Nearly all the animals of Antarctica live near the ocean and must return there to survive the winter or find food. The only animals that live permanently on land are tiny insects and mites.

Polar Ecosystems

Just like in any other biome, the organisms of the polar biomes depend on each other to survive. The community of plants, animals, and other organisms, together with their physical environment, make up what we call an ecosystem. Nearly all Earth's ecosystems are maintained by energy from the sun. Plants or algae use the sun's energy to make food, so they can grow and reproduce. Herbivores (plant-eating animals) eat the plants, and carnivores (flesh-eating animals) eat the herbivores. So the food made by the plants passes along a food chain, from plant to herbivore to carnivore.

The ecosystems of the Arctic and Antarctic are unusual. In Antarctica there are very few land plants, so most animals depend on food from the oceans. The base of the food chain is made up of phytoplankton—microscopic, plantlike organisms that live on the surface of the ocean. These are eaten by zooplankton—tiny organisms that live in the surface water. The zooplankton are eaten by fish, squid, mollusks, and other animals, and these provide food for penguins and seals.

Being a warmer and less extreme place than Antarctica, the Arctic is home to many more species. Just as in Antarctica, there is a marine food chain based on phytoplankton. This food chain is very important for animals that come on land to breed, such as seabirds, seals, and walruses. But there is also a land-based food chain. At the bottom of the chain are lichens, algae, and land plants. At the top are meat eaters, including wolves, snowy owls, polar bears, and people. In between comes everything from bumblebees and wolf spiders to caribou.

 ## Midget Giants

The largest antarctic animal that lives permanently on land is a wingless relative of insects called a springtail. It grows to only half an inch (13 mm) long. The continent's biggest native land predator is a mite—a tiny spiderlike creature. It weighs less than a hundred thousandth of an ounce (0.0001 g).

In Antarctica, there are hardly any land plants. Nearly all the animals that live there, such as these chinstrap penguins, live off food from the ocean, such as fish. These penguins are resting on an unusual iceberg made of blue ice.

Life in the Freezer

If you took a monkey from a rain forest and moved it to Antarctica, it would die very quickly. Monkeys are well adapted to the heat and moisture of the tropics, but they cannot survive in a polar desert. All the creatures that live in the polar regions have evolved special characteristics, or adaptations, that help them survive there.

The biggest challenge is staying warm. Many polar animals are warm-blooded. Just like people, they keep a constant body temperature, no matter how the temperature of their surroundings varies. Being warm-blooded allows animals to stay active even when their surroundings are freezing cold. In contrast, cold-blooded animals, such as lizards and frogs, would become inactive and freeze—so it is not surprising that very few lizards or frogs venture into the Arctic, and none can be found in Antarctica.

Warm-blooded animals need features that stop them from losing heat. Most warm-blooded animals have layers of insulation around their body to retain heat. People insulate themselves with clothes, but other

animals, such as polar bears, have a thick fur coat. They also have a layer of fat, or blubber. The blubber acts mainly as an energy store for times when food is hard to find, but it also helps keep in the heat. Seals and walruses also have blubber, but unlike land animals, they have an extra insulating feature. By changing their blood flow, they can keep their blubber layer cool while maintaining a warm temperature deep inside their body. Walruses have so much blubber that they risk overheating when they come onto land.

Arctic foxes, like polar bears, have a thick, layered, insulating coat of fur. The fur holds a layer of warm air around the body and acts as a barrier to cold.

Walruses rest on land a great deal. This way, they spend less energy keeping their body warm in the cold sea. They can use their tusks as picks during fights.

Although they spend much of their time in the ocean, walruses come ashore to rest and breed in large colonies on the Arctic coast. To lose heat, they blush—blood flows through the skin, turning their body bright pink.

Walruses use their long whiskers to feel for shellfish on the murky seafloor. With their tusks held out of the way, they grub about for food in the mud, a bit like pigs do. And just as submarines can push their way through sea ice, so a walrus can use its tough head to bash through ice up to 8 inches (20 cm) thick.

 # Cold Feet

Keeping their feet warm is a particular problem for polar animals. Most of an animal's warmth is in the center of its body. Any body parts that stick out from the center, such as legs, arms, ears, and a nose, are the first to lose heat in cold weather. To save precious heat energy, some animals have legs that can be colder than the rest of their body. Seagulls and caribou are two examples. Eskimos have long known that the lower parts of a caribou's leg freeze at much lower temperatures than the upper parts. For this reason, they would use the fat from caribou feet to oil the strings of their bows.

Big Is Better?

A 19th-century scientist named Carl Bergmann claimed that bigger creatures are better off in cold climates than smaller ones, because they don't lose heat so quickly. Why should this be so? The amount of heat an object can hold depends on its volume (the space it takes up), while the speed it loses heat depends on the area (size) of its surface. Small animals have a higher ratio of surface area to volume, so they lose heat faster. Think how slowly a hot potato cools down, compared to a similar volume of peas. The peas have more surface area than the potato, so they turn cold much quicker. But size is not the only answer to surviving at the poles. A large animal must find more food to fuel itself than smaller animals, even in winter, when food is hard to find. In addition, small animals can better avoid the cold by staying in burrows.

Sometimes fur and blubber are not enough to beat the cold. The musk oxen of the arctic tundra and the penguins of Antarctica may huddle together to help stay warm. Ptarmigan and small birds fly into fluffy snow banks, or dig themselves into the snow of the tundra with their feet. Cold as this may seem, it is still warmer than standing in a blizzard. Some polar animals have a particular size or shape that helps them cope with the cold. Large, bulky animals generally stand up to the cold better than small animals, for example.

Migrating Mammals

Rather than endure the dark and freezing tundra winter, most caribou migrate south at the end of summer. Every year, more than a million of these arctic deer make a long trek to the forests of the taiga, where they find shelter in winter. They return to the tundra on the arctic coastal plains in spring, when

These reindeer live in Siberia, which has some of the coldest winters the Arctic has to offer. It is no wonder, then, that the reindeer migrate south into the taiga biome, shown here, to find shelter in winter.

they give birth to their calves. Caribou live throughout the tundra and taiga of North America, Europe, and Russia, though they are called reindeer in Europe and Russia. The Peary caribou and the Svalbard reindeer live on arctic islands, so they can't move south to escape the winter. They must endure the dark and cold, but when desperate, they attempt dangerous crossings over the sea ice.

Another arctic mammal, the musk ox, does not migrate far, but shifts only a few miles between its summer and winter grazing grounds. In summer, musk oxen eat sedges and willows on low-lying tundra; in winter, they move to ground free of deep snow to eat grasses exposed by the arctic winds. The severe climate is seldom a problem for musk oxen, because their shaggy coats are eight times warmer than sheep's fur and protect them well against harsh blizzards. The most severe blizzards can last for several days, though, and prevent musk oxen from feeding. At such times, they lie down together to deflect the wind. One way musk oxen lower their need for food in winter is to spend little time moving. The less energy they use for movement, the more energy they have to maintain their body temperature.

Hibernating Mammals

The musk ox's method of saving its energy is halfway between staying active for the winter and hibernating completely. To hibernate fully, animals seek shelter, reduce their body temperature, and become inactive, or dormant, usually until the winter has passed. During hibernation, their heart beats more slowly and they breathe much less often than they do normally. Although they don't eat, their body survives on reserves of stored fat.

Right: On the treeless tundra, there is nowhere for arctic ground squirrels to hide. This one is keeping a lookout for predators while others in its group feed.

Grizzly bears hibernate in large dens that they construct of snow in the autumn. With its entrance tunnel, small living room, and air hole, a bear's den can be a cozy place to spend the winter. The snow keeps out the cold, and the bear's body heat (and that of its cubs) keeps the den warm. A bear also prepares for hibernation by building up the fat on its body. The fat provides water as well as food for the long winter months.

The grizzly bear is one of the largest hibernating mammals in the Arctic. Much smaller mammals hibernate, too, including the arctic ground squirrel, which spends two thirds of every year in hibernation.

Arctic ground squirrels don't live in trees (there aren't any) but in underground burrows. These provide shelter from predators as well as from the cold climate. Lots of animals prey on the ground squirrel—snowy owls hunt them from above, and polar bears try to claw the squirrels out of their holes. The ground squirrel's hibernation is made up of short periods. During a period, it curls into a ball and allows its body temperature to fall to that of its burrow. If its burrow gets very cold, the squirrel's body might freeze solid, so its brain stays awake and keeps its body temperature above the freezing point.

South polar skuas are vicious predators. Their favorite food is penguin chick, but they also eat other seabirds and sometimes even other skuas' chicks.

A flight of snow geese might be a familiar sight as far south as Mexico, but their destination is the arctic tundra, where they raise their chicks in summer.

All mammals need sleep, so after two weeks or so, the squirrel warms itself to normal body temperature, relaxes, and falls asleep for some hours, before entering its next period of wakeful hibernation.

Migrating Birds

Just as some people fly to warmer places for winter, so birds use their wings to escape the worst of the weather. Most arctic birds spend only their breeding season in the tundra, and fly vast distances south once they have raised their young. The sandpiper, for example, flies 12,000 miles (19,000 km) south from its arctic nesting grounds, which is like flying from New York to Los Angeles four times. The bird with the most spectacular migration pattern is the arctic tern. It spends the winter

 ## Goodbye, Great Auk

When European ships started to visit the Arctic, one of the first casualties was the great auk. Similar to a penguin, this flightless bird was very common on islands off Newfoundland. From the 16th century onward, sailors began to kill the great auk because it was a quick and easy source of food, oil, and feathers. Numbers of the birds plummeted. By the 18th century, the Newfoundland government was trying to halt the massive slaughter. But it was already too late. In June 1844, collectors clubbed the last two great auks to death for their eggs, and the bird became extinct.

in the ocean around Antarctica. In summer, it flies all the way to its breeding grounds in the arctic tundra.

About 50 species of birds thrive south of the antarctic circle, including terns, petrels, fulmars, gulls, shearwaters, and albatrosses. In Antarctica, the birds live along the coast because they depend on the sea for food. Most antarctic birds eat shrimplike animals called krill, fish, or squid, but some eat other birds or even seals. Petrels loiter around seabird colonies, hoping to gobble up a penguin chick or feast on a dead seal. But even petrels live in fear of skuas—aggressive

Early summer in the Russian Arctic is time for red-breasted geese to arrive and begin nesting.

 ## Penguin Points

▲ Penguins live in the Antarctic but not the Arctic.

▲ Penguins can't fly. They use their wings as flippers for swimming.

▲ Penguins have no need to fly because there are no large land predators in the Antarctic.

▲ Fossils found in New Zealand reveal that some prehistoric penguins were as tall as people.

▲ The only penguins to nest on the antarctic mainland are Adélie penguins (below) and emperor penguins.

birds that terrorize seabird colonies and readily attack people when threatened.

More birds live in the Arctic than Antarctica. There are several reasons for this: the arctic tundra is nearer to other areas of land; the climate is less harsh; and there are more varied habitats for breeding and feeding. Even so, most birds fly south for the winter and spend just a few months breeding in the Arctic each summer. There are only a few hardy year-round residents, including the ptarmigan, the snowy owl, and the raven.

During the breeding season, predators are common in the Arctic, both in the air and on the ground. Airborne predators include eagles and skuas, while land predators include foxes, wolves, bears, and ermines (short-tailed arctic weasels).

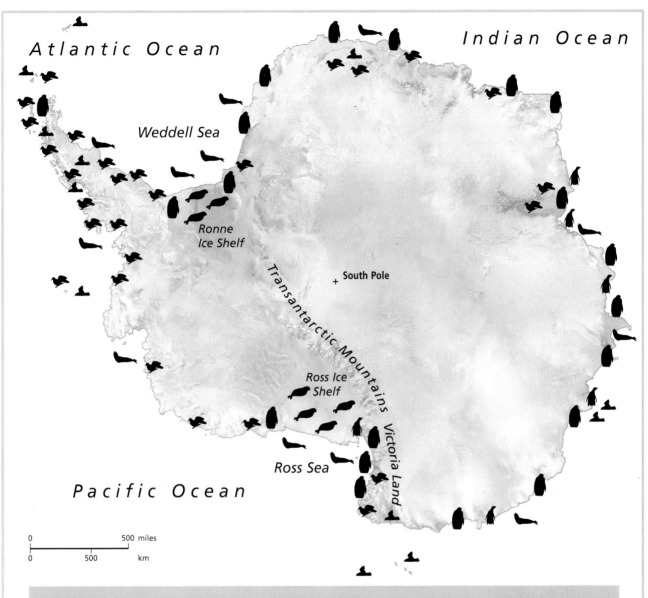

Atlantic Ocean

Indian Ocean

Weddell Sea

Ronne
Ice Shelf

Transantarctic Mountains

+ South Pole

Victoria Land

Ross Ice
Shelf

Ross Sea

Pacific Ocean

| 0 | | 500 miles |
| 0 | 500 | km |

Animals of Antarctica

Most of Antarctica is covered with a high dome of ice. Nothing can live on top—it is much too cold and too far from the nearest source of food: the ocean. All antarctic animals live within reach of the ocean. Large colonies of Adélie and emperor penguins roost on rocky coasts and islands around Antarctica. In winter, though, male emperor penguins travel far from the open sea across the ice to incubate

their eggs in safety. Predatory birds such as petrels and skuas hunt and scavenge near the coastal penguins, but some fly inland to nest in dry valleys and on outcrops of rock. Ross seals live deep in fields of sea ice, but Weddell seals live even farther from the open sea, on the permanently frozen ice shelves. They reach the sea by cutting down through the ice with their teeth.

 Adélie
penguin

 Emperor
penguin

 Ross
seal

 Weddell
seal

 South polar
skua

 Snow
petrel

37

Because there are lots of predators, arctic birds need effective defenses. Fulmars vomit on their attackers. Arctic swans trample, bite, batter, and hiss at anything that threatens them. And many birds nest together in large colonies, from ducks to guillemots. With so many eyes and ears on the alert in a colony, the risk of being caught unawares by an attacker is much lower.

For migrating birds, timing is everything. They must carefully time their transglobal journeys so they arrive at their breeding grounds at exactly the right time of year. Timing is important in other ways, too. Skuas lay their eggs so the chicks hatch at the same time as those of penguins. This ensures there will be plenty of food around for the hungry young skuas.

Toughest of the Tough

Although some polar creatures shy away from winter by migrating or hibernating, others remain where they are, using a variety of different tricks to survive. Unable to fly away from Antarctica, penguins huddle together to keep warm. The ptarmigan is one of the few arctic birds that doesn't fly south for the winter. It also holds the record for the bird that spends winter closest to the North Pole. When winter approaches, the ptarmigan changes from brown to white and sprouts fluffy feathers on its feet. Its uses its feathered feet to dig tunnels in the snow, where it is much warmer than in the air outside.

Lemmings endure the arctic winter by digging a complicated network of tunnels in the snow. As they dig down to the ground

Starvation Wages

After a female emperor penguin lays her egg, she leaves it to the male to care for. Balancing the egg on his feet, the male tucks a flap of bare skin over the egg to keep it warm. He spends more than three months of the bitter Antarctic winter without eating while he looks after the egg. By huddling together (below), the male penguins can limit their heat loss during this time. Even so, they lose half their body weight in these months.

White in Winter

Many polar creatures are white, including polar bears, Dall's sheep, Peary caribou, and some gyrfalcons. Others turn white only when the winter comes. These include arctic hares (left and right), ermines, lemmings, arctic foxes, and birds such as the ptarmigan. Being white helps animals hide in snow or ice, and so reduces the chance of being spotted by a predator. It also helps predators sneak up on victims without being seen. Some scientists think that white fur is warmer than other colors. White materials reflect heat more than dark materials, so a coat of white fur reflects body heat back toward the skin. The white hairs also contain air spaces that make them even warmer.

surface, they eat whatever plants they find. Similar to hamsters, they have short legs and ears, and lots of brown fur. But in winter they turn white, like many arctic creatures. Lemmings breed very quickly—females give birth to up to nine young at a time, only three weeks after mating. Sometimes the population of lemmings grows so much that many are forced to leave their burrows and migrate elsewhere. The mass migrations happen every few years, when hundreds of lemmings can be seen scampering across the tundra. Occasionally, some fall off cliffs or drown in ponds or the sea by accident, but lemmings do not do this deliberately, as some people think.

Like any other biome, the arctic tundra has scavengers—animals that live off the spoils of others. The arctic fox, for instance, follows polar bears for the remains of their kills. Well-adapted to life in the cold, it has a short nose and small ears that reduce heat

Lemmings survive the arctic winter by gnawing plants, which they find beneath the snow.

loss. Its fur is luxurious and even covers the undersides of its feet to keep out the cold. The polar bears it follows are also expert arctic survivors, equally at home on land, on sea ice, or swimming in the chilly ocean. Polar bears prey on seals and young walruses and also scavenge from dead whales. If food is in short supply, they venture inland for berries, grass, or whatever they can find. Some polar bears even enter towns to sniff out morsels of food in garbage.

Polar Warriors

Suppose you had to design an animal to survive life at the North Pole. Could you come up with anything better than a polar bear? A typical polar bear is about 7 feet (2.1 m) tall and 1,200 pounds (540 kg) in weight—as much as five heavyweight wrestlers.

A lot of this weight is fat. Underneath the skin, polar bears have a blanket of blubber several inches deep. It is thickest on the back of the legs and the hind quarters, where the animal is most exposed to the wind. Although blubber is helpful for keeping the bear warm as it plods over the ice, it is even more important when the bear is paddling through the water. Polar

bears are excellent swimmers—they can swim 60 miles (100 km) across open water to reach the ice floes where they hunt.

Blubber is only one layer of the bear's clothing. Next comes a cozy layer of wool. And on the outside, there is a thick fur coat made up of long, hard guard hairs. Each guard hair works like one of the glass fibers in a fiber-optic cable. Sunlight is carried down the hair to the bear's body, helping warm the skin. With blubber, wool, and a sun-heated fur coat, polar bears are so well-insulated that they hardly show up on infrared (heat-sensitive) cameras.

No Way In

Creatures that develop ways of defending themselves against their hunters are more likely to thrive. When musk oxen are attacked, they huddle together in a circle, rump-to-rump, protecting their calves between them. That leaves just their heads and their horns exposed, which makes it much easier to defend themselves against predators such as wolves.

Small Is Beautiful

Cold conditions may favor large creatures, but the polar regions are also home to many small forms of life. One of the Arctic's most ferocious little creatures is a shrimplike animal called an amphipod, which lives in the ocean. When a young Eskimo fell through the ice and drowned in the Canadian Arctic some years ago, rescuers were shocked when they discovered his dead body. Although his clothes were intact, amphipods had picked off and eaten all the flesh from his bones in less than a day.

Lots of insects and spiders live in the arctic tundra. They spend the winter in resting form, usually as eggs, which are not killed by freezing. As soon as it is warm enough, the insects burst into activity. Mosquitoes hatch from tundra pools and swarm in millions. There are so many mosquitoes that this may be one of the reasons why caribou migrate north to give birth. The insects live both in the taiga, where caribou spend their winters, and in the tundra, where caribou calve. But they appear a whole month later in the tundra. This extra month gives the caribou time to calve and raise their young before the mosquitoes start biting. The multitude of other arctic insects includes butterflies, crane flies, and bumblebees.

Plants and insects must rush to take advantage of the brief arctic summer. This crane fly is soaking up some sunshine on an arctic poppy.

Antarctica

Antarctica is the coldest, driest, windiest, darkest, and highest continent on Earth. Nowhere on the planet is less hospitable to life.

Most of Antarctica is covered by ice so thick that only mountaintops show through it.

Fact File

▲ Antarctica has 70% of Earth's freshwater but is one of the world's driest deserts.

▲ In winter, Antarctica doubles in size as the sea freezes around it.

▲ On average, Antarctica is three times higher than other continents because of all the ice. The weight of the ice has squashed the land to below sea level in some places.

▲ Antarctica's ice is slowly moving. It takes about 50,000 years for a snowflake at the South Pole to get to the ocean.

1. Lambert Glacier
A vast glacier that flows slowly off the mainland and into Amery Ice Shelf.

2. Vostok
This Russian base is officially the coldest place on Earth. The world's lowest ever temperature (−128.6°F or −89.2°C) was recorded there.

3. South Magnetic Pole
The place on Earth's surface that compasses point away from. The magnetic poles slowly change position over time.

4. Dry Valleys
Ice-free, rocky valleys near the Transantarctic Mountains.

5. McMurdo Station
This U.S. base on Ross Island is Antarctica's biggest community, with a summer population of 1,200 and a winter population of 200.

6. Mount Erebus
A gigantic active volcano on Ross Island, at the edge of the Ross Ice Shelf.

7. Transantarctic Mountains
This vast mountain range forms the dividing line between Greater and Lesser Antarctica.

8. South Pole
The most southerly point on Earth.

9. Ross Ice Shelf
A vast shelf of permanent sea ice that ends in towering cliffs.

10. Vinson Massif
Antarctica's tallest mountain, at 16,864 feet (5,140 m)—a popular destination for climbers.

11. Antarctic Peninsula
The northernmost point of Antarctica. The Peninsula contains many islands and volcanoes, some of which are active.

The Dry Valleys

It's strange to think that a continent with as much ice as Antarctica could also contain a rocky desert, yet the Dry Valleys have been free of ice for millions of years. They are dry because the nearby mountains hold back glaciers, and because strong winds blow away what little snow falls.

Despite the name, the Dry Valleys contain Antarctica's only river—the Onyx—which flows only in summer and contains beautifully clear water. There are also a few lakes, though these are permanently frozen over.

You might think the Dry Valleys would be devoid of life, but they aren't. The rocks contain microscopic organisms called cyanobacteria, which can lie dormant for hundreds of years. When enough snow falls to make the rocks damp, the cyanobacteria spring back to life, using the sun's energy to make food.

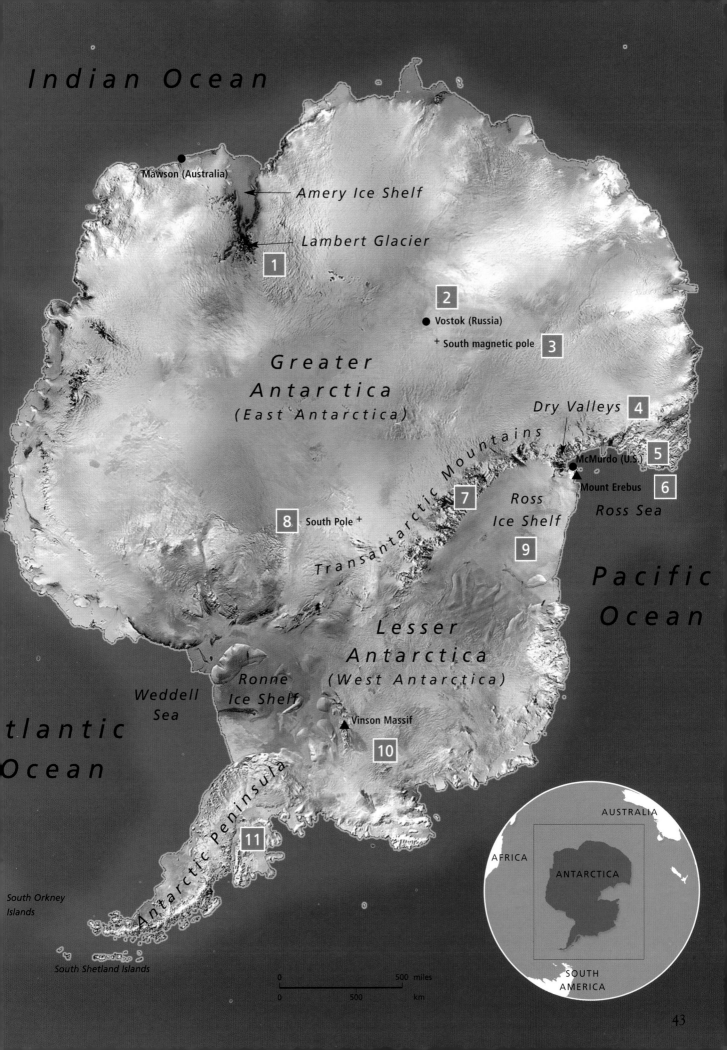

Indian Ocean

Mawson (Australia)

Amery Ice Shelf

Lambert Glacier

1

2

● Vostok (Russia)

+ South magnetic pole   3

Greater
Antarctica
(East Antarctica)

Dry Valleys   4

Transantarctic Mountains

McMurdo (U.S.)   5

▲ Mount Erebus   6

7   Ross
Ice Shelf   Ross Sea

8   South Pole +   9

Pacific
Ocean

Lesser
Antarctica
(West Antarctica)

Weddell
Sea   Ronne
Ice Shelf

Vinson Massif ▲

10

Atlantic
Ocean

Antarctic Peninsula

11

South Orkney
Islands

South Shetland Islands

0   500 miles

0   500   km

AUSTRALIA

AFRICA   ANTARCTICA

SOUTH
AMERICA

People and the Poles

Antarctica has always been too cold and desolate for anyone other than scientists and explorers to consider living there, but the Arctic is another matter. People have lived within the arctic circle for thousands of years.

The people who have lived in the Arctic for longest are often called Eskimos. Language experts think the word *eskimo* probably came from the Algonquian language, from a word meaning "she laces a snowshoe." Other language experts claim Eskimo means "eater of raw meat." Some arctic people do not like being described in this way, because it seems to imply that they lead simple and primitive lives.

Instead, different Eskimo groups prefer different names. People from the eastern part of the Canadian Arctic are called Inuit, which means "the people." One member of the Inuit is called an Inuk. People from the North Slope of Alaska are called Inupiat, while those who live around the Bering Sea prefer to be called Yupik. In Siberia live arctic people called Chukchi and Nenet. In this book, we use the word Eskimo to refer to all the native peoples of the Arctic.

The inhabitants of Savissivik in northwestern Greenland talk to the rest of the world with the help of this communications dish.

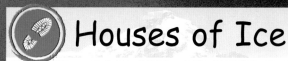 Houses of Ice

In the Inuit language, the word *igloo* simply means "house." People often imagine Eskimos living in ice igloos—houses made from blocks of ice or snow. But ice igloos are only temporary dwellings used by hunters and travelers in winter—people never spent the entire year in them. Eskimos built more permanent igloos from stones or wood, covered with grass and sometimes lined with animal skins. At fishing and hunting sites, they lived in tents made from animal skins. For bedding, they built a bench out of earth or snow and topped it with heather or moss to make it comfortable. Then they covered it with a rug made from animal skins, which stopped the bed melting and kept the sleeper warm.

The Eskimo Life

People have lived in the Arctic lands of Europe, Asia, and North America for at least 4,000 years. Like other Native Americans, Eskimos reached North America by crossing the Bering Strait from Asia. They may have walked across a land bridge that once connected Russia to Alaska, or they may have come by boat. If so, they probably used wooden boats similar to the umiak that they use today. These were traditionally covered with animal hide and often rowed by women.

Fish dried on a rack (above) can be kept until winter, when they provide huskies (below) with energy to pull sleds.

The Eskimo way of life has changed a lot,
but in the past it consisted largely of hunting
and fishing. With so few plants in the Arctic,
meat was the most important source of food.
Eskimos studied the changing seasons and the
crafty hunting habits of polar bears. They
knew how to catch fish, whales, and
seals—and how to keep warm.
Most of all, they knew how
to survive in one of the
harshest places
on Earth.

Polar Ships

Explorers first sailed to the Arctic in wooden ships. Though sturdy in the open sea, the ships were no match for the treacherous polar ocean. Many ships were crushed like matchsticks as the ice closed in around them. Others crashed into icebergs and were never seen again. Today, steel ships called icebreakers (right) can slice passages through ice, and large submarines are strong enough to break through as they surface. But every captain knows the story of the *Titanic*—the passenger liner that sank in 1912 after hitting an iceberg—and treats the polar oceans with the respect they deserve.

Conquering the Poles

In the 16th century, European sailors began exploring the Arctic. They wanted to find a shortcut from the Atlantic to Asia—the Northwest Passage (see map). Many of the early explorers are remembered in the names of places around the North Pole.

Frobisher Bay and Baffin Island, for example, are named for English sailors Martin Frobisher (1535–1594) and William Baffin (1584–1622). In 1616, Baffin sailed farther north than anyone had ever gone, and his record lasted more than 200 years. The Davis Strait is named for English sailor John Davis (1550–1605), who explored the seas around Greenland and Labrador. The Bering Strait is named for Danish sailor Vitus Bering (1680–1741). He was the first European to prove that Alaska and Siberia are not joined.

In 1819, an English explorer named William Parry (1790–1855) sailed almost all the way to the north magnetic pole, mapping out a large area of the Arctic as he did so. He is now remembered at the Parry Channel and Parry Islands. Parry once kept his sailors amused by building a billiard table out of blocks of snow and walrus skin.

The North Pole

Perhaps the greatest feat of Arctic exploration was achieved by the U.S. explorer Robert Edwin Peary (1856–1920). One of his

Polar explorers and scientists must endure air so cold that it freezes the water droplets in their breath.

The Northwest Passage

Scale: 0–500 miles, 0–500 km

ALASKA

Bering Strait

ASIA

Arctic Ocean

CANADA

Victoria Island

Parry Islands

RUSSIA

+ North Pole

Hudson Bay

Ellesmere Island

Frobisher Bay

Baffin Island

Baffin Bay

+ North magnetic pole's position in 1819

Labrador

Davis Strait

GREENLAND

Atlantic Ocean

In the 16th century, explorers began searching for a new trade route to China and India. Those who discovered this fabled route, called the Northwest Passage, would earn a fortune in the spice trade. One after another, though, early explorers turned back in faliure. When Roald Amundsen eventually found the Northwest Passage, he found it to be extremely difficult to pass. The voyage lasted three years, including two winters trapped in the ice.

Martin Frobisher, 1576   *John Davis, 1585*

William Baffin, 1616   *Roald Amundsen, 1903–06*

first successes was to prove that Greenland was an island, not a continent. After exploring the Arctic for many years, he made several attempts to reach the North Pole. He finally accomplished this—one of the world's greatest challenges—in 1909. There was some doubt about whether Peary had reached the pole first, because another explorer, U.S. doctor Frederick Albert Cook, claimed to have beaten him. Cook's records later proved to be false, and Peary was declared the victor.

It was another two years before anyone reached the South Pole. Two teams of explorers, one from Britain and one from

Norway, raced for victory through the harsh conditions of Antarctica. The Norwegian team was led by Roald Amundsen (1872–1928), who had wanted to be the first man to reach the North Pole. When Robert Peary beat him to it, Amundsen decided to head for Antarctica instead. Wisely, he chose to use dogsleds to pull his team's heavy packs, while the British team, led by Robert Scott (1868–1912), hauled their sleds by hand. Amundsen won the race, reaching the South Pole in December 1911. Scott's party arrived one month later, but all five members of the team perished on their way back home.

Although Amundsen reached the pole first, both of these courageous men are remembered on the noticeboard that marks the South Pole today. Amundsen later tried to reach the North Pole by sea and by airplane. He died in a plane crash in 1928 trying to rescue another explorer who had vanished at the North Pole.

The World of the Modern Eskimo

Since the poles were conquered, people have exploited the Arctic and Antarctica much more, and life for the Eskimo peoples has changed forever. Once isolated from the rest of the world, their lives today are much more like those of people anywhere.

Inuksuit

Eskimos are well-known for their intricate carvings, but they also make huge sculptures by piling up stones or boulders. Each one of these is called an inuksuk, and together they are called inuksuit. Inuksuk means "looking like a man," and some of these rough stone sculptures do seem to have arms and legs. Sometimes inuksuit were used as signposts or markers in the tundra. An inuksuk might show where the hunting was good, for instance, or it might help Eskimos guide herds of caribou. Some people would leave offerings next to them before making hazardous journeys.

Transportation has changed a great deal for the Eskimo peoples. Where they once got around on foot or with dogsleds, today they are more likely to use snowmobiles (motorbikes on skis) or pick-up trucks.

Right: Between May and August, the sun never sets at the town of Uummannaq, on the west coast of Greenland.

Above: Hunters in the Arctic are more likely to use snowmobiles than dogsleds today. Tents provide temporary homes during hunting trips.

Not everything has changed, though. Eskimos still use the large boats called umiak, but today these are more likely to be driven by a gas-powered outboard motor than paddled with oars.

Technology has transformed the way Eskimos hunt. Traditionally they threw long harpoons to kill polar bears, seals, and other animals. Because the harpoons were made from wood, they floated and were easy to retrieve from the sea. Today, Eskimos are just as likely to use a rifle with a telescopic sight. Although many Eskimos try hard to maintain their hunting way of life, many people today buy their food in stores.

We often still think of Eskimos wearing fur coats and huddling around fires inside their ice igloos. But an Eskimo's home today is a world away from snow houses and animal-skin tents. Although some people still use igloos or tents on hunting trips, many now live in modern, timber-framed houses with central heating. Because their communities are small and remote, Eskimos today often use the Internet, both to keep in touch with each other and to make contact with people elsewhere in the world. Many also use citizens' band (CB) radios to pass news to friends and relatives.

Where Did All the Eskimos Go?

People build up resistance to diseases over a long period of time. When two different peoples meet, one may bring diseases to which the other has no defense. This happened when Europeans began to trade regularly with the Eskimos. Besides giving the Eskimos valuable goods, the Europeans gave them smallpox, tuberculosis (TB), and diptheria. Since Eskimos have lower immunity to these diseases, huge numbers died, sometimes leaving whole villages empty. This is one reason why there are fewer Eskimos in the Arctic today.

Who Owns Antarctica?

Geologists think that Antarctica may contain huge amounts of oil, gas, coal, and other valuable minerals. For this reason, a number of different nations have tried to claim parts of the antarctic continent. However, none of these claims have been recognized by the international community.

Instead, 12 nations signed an agreement called the Antarctic Treaty, which says that no one can develop Antarctica. The treaty came into force in 1961 and bans oil and mineral exploration for at least 50 years. Since 1961, a further 28 nations have signed the treaty. All these nations agree that Antarctica should be used for peaceful scientific research only. But this does not mean Antarctica is completely protected. The countries that signed the treaty could agree to rewrite it at any time.

Eskimo Culture

Eskimos were good at making the best of the things that surrounded them. They knew how to transform caribou into clothes or boots, and how to make bedding from the hair of musk oxen.

They turned bird skins inside out to make slippers, and put fur on the soles of their boots to walk silently when hunting. Polar bears have fur on the soles of their feet for the same reason. Today, of course, many Eskimos prefer to wear anoraks and boots made in factories.

Eskimo life has changed in many ways, through contact with other peoples and with the arrival of modern technology. Some of the changes have made life easier for the Eskimos. Others, such as diseases carried by European sailors, have threatened their very existence.

Although early Arctic explorers believed the Eskimos were simple people, they were advanced in many ways. The first Eskimo settlers arrived in North America with pottery, lamps, needles, and sophisticated ivory tools. Archaeologists (people who study past civilizations) have found remains of these items in the places where Eskimos once lived. The ancient Eskimos' tools

The Chukchi people live in east Siberia, across the Bering Sea from Alaska. Some were reindeer herders while others hunted sea mammals. This Chukchi girl is dancing around her animal-skin tent, called a yarang.

and their knowledge of animals and plants were very important in allowing them to thrive in the Arctic.

Eskimos have always had a lively culture. Much of it is based on their life as a hunting people. Their harpoons were often highly decorated with intricate patterns. Since ancient times, they have carved little figures of the animals they hunted from ivory, soapstone, and wood.

Eskimos do not hunt all the time—they also like to relax and enjoy themselves. Singing and dancing are very important in Eskimo communities, and huge feasts are regular events. In Alaska, hunters hold a joyous celebration at the end of every whaling season. The person who catches the most whale meat is flung up and down on a trampoline made out of walrus hide stretched over whale ribs.

Antarctic Science

Many people live in the Arctic, but hardly anyone lives inside the antarctic circle. Apart from a few thousand tourists who visit Antarctica each year, the only exceptions are scientists who live in some 60 research bases. The bases are dotted around the continent. There are even some on top of the ice cap, such as the U.S. base at the South Pole (above).

Not all the scientists who study Antarctica are based there. Some research the continent from laboratories in places such as Great Britain and the United States. Polar animals tagged with radio transmitters can be tracked by satellite and studied from anywhere on Earth. The animals may have to endure the harsh polar winter, but the scientists can stay warm back at their home bases.

Scientists are not only interested in the plants and animals of Antarctica. They also want to understand the climate of this unusual place and how it can affect weather over the rest of the planet. Today, Antarctica's scientists are studying the atmosphere and the ice, and tackling two of Earth's biggest problems: the ozone hole and global warming.

Greenland

Greenland contains very little in the way of green land. Three quarters of the country lies inside the arctic circle, and most of it is a polar desert, covered in ice. The few people who live in Greenland inhabit the tundra regions around the coast of the country.

Greenland Facts

▲ The ice on Greenland is, on average, almost a mile (1.6 km) thick. The weight of all the ice has made the land underneath sag below sea level.

▲ Greenland was given its name by Eric the Red, a Norwegian explorer. He thought that if he made the country sound like a nice place, people would want to move there from Iceland.

▲ Today, Greenland's official name is Kalaallit Nunaat, which means "Greenlander's Country." The country has ruled itself since 1979.

Icebergs locked in the frozen sea lie in Meteorite Bay in northwestern Greenland. The village of Savissivik is icebound for most of the year. A boat brings its supplies once a year, in August.

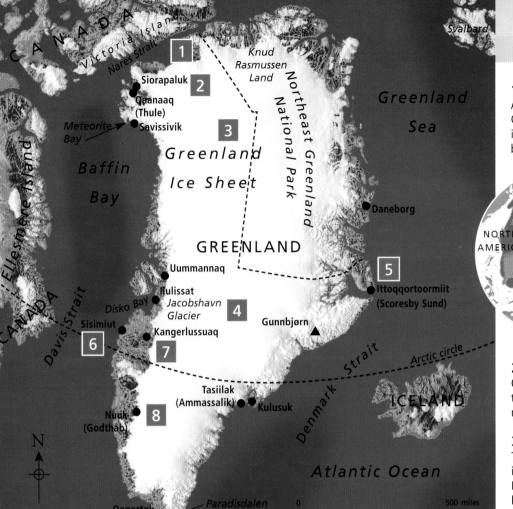

Map labels

- C A N A D A
- Victoria Island
- Nares Strait
- Svalbard
- **1**
- Siorapaluk **2**
- Qaanaaq (Thule)
- Knud Rasmussen Land
- Meteorite Bay
- Savissivik
- **3**
- Greenland Ice Sheet
- Northeast Greenland National Park
- Greenland Sea
- Baffin Bay
- Ellesmere Island
- CANADA
- Daneborg
- GREENLAND
- Uummannaq
- Ilulissat
- Jacobshavn Glacier
- Disko Bay
- **4**
- **5**
- Ittoqqortoormiit (Scoresby Sund)
- Sisimiut
- Davis Strait
- **6**
- Kangerlussuaq **7**
- Gunnbjørn
- Arctic circle
- Denmark Strait
- Tasiilak (Ammassalik)
- Kulusuk
- ICELAND
- Nuuk (Godthåb) **8**
- N
- Atlantic Ocean
- Qaqortok
- Paradisdalen
- Nanortalik **9**
- 0   500 miles
- 0   500 km

World map inset

- ASIA
- NORTH AMERICA
- EUROPE

The World's Biggest National Park

The enormous Greenland National Park is the largest protected area for wildlife in the world. With numerous different habitats, including tundra, fjords, glaciers, lakes, and rivers, the park is home to many different animals and birds. The animal residents include polar bears, caribou, walruses, musk oxen, and wolves. Among the birds are the snowy owl and the gyrfalcon, a gray-white bird of prey found in much of the Arctic.

No people are allowed to live in the park, but native people from the town of Ittoqqortoormiit are still permitted to hunt there. Because there are no roads, visitors get around by dogsled.

1. Nares Strait
A narrow sea passage between Greenland and Ellesmere Island in Canada. The strait is often bridged by sea ice.

2. Siorapaluk
Only 846 miles (1,362 km) from the North Pole, this is the northernmost village on Earth.

3. Greenland Ice Sheet
This is the world's second-largest ice sheet, after Antarctica's. It covers 85 percent of the land in Greenland.

4. Jakobshavn Glacier
The Jakobshavn Glacier flows up to 100 feet (30 m) a day as it moves away from the Greenland Ice Sheet, making it one of the world's fastest glaciers.

5. Ittoqqortoormiit
This small town borders the world's largest national park and the world's largest fjord.

6. Sisimiut
Greenland's second-largest town contains the country's only outdoor swimming pool.

7. Kangerlussuaq
A long fjord on the west coast, where the country's main airport is located.

8. Nuuk
The capital of Greenland (also known as Godthåb).

9. Paradisdalen
An important nature reserve containing the only woodland in Greenland.

The Future

The poles were once remote enough to escape the influence of the modern world. Now, climate change, industry, and pollution all threaten to change the polar biomes forever.

People once believed that Earth was a vast place of wild beauty. No matter what they did to it or how much they took out of it, the planet would always heal itself and recover. Today, few places remain untouched by human activities, and Earth seems a much smaller planet than it used to. From coral reefs to tropical forests, many habitats are under threat of destruction. The polar regions, which are among the most remote places on Earth, are among the most threatened. No one knows what the future holds for the Arctic and Antarctica, or whether these ice-covered worlds will even exist in the coming centuries.

The Warming World

Earth's climate warms up and cools down naturally over the centuries. In the past, there have been many ice ages, when huge parts of the sea froze over, and many interglacials (periods between the ice ages), when everything warmed up again. Today,

Earth's climate is changing for a different reason. Scientists believe Earth is heating up because of carbon dioxide and other gases released into the atmosphere by people.

Carbon dioxide forms when we burn fossil fuels, such as gasoline or coal. The gas acts like the glass in a greenhouse, trapping heat inside Earth's atmosphere and gradually making the temperature rise. Although global

warming could change the whole of the planet, it threatens the polar regions especially, and the plants, animals, and people who live there.

Global warming means that the world as a whole becomes warmer. In places such as New York or Los Angeles, that does not only mean that the days are warmer. The weather could be more intense—there could be more heatwaves, floods, and droughts. But for the polar regions, global warming could be disastrous. As the world warms up, the ice on Antarctica and Greenland might begin to melt. Meltwater running into the sea

Melting glaciers crash into the sea at Kenai Fjords National Park, Alaska. Such glaciers will disappear altogether if Earth's climate gets much warmer.

would raise sea levels around the world, causing low-lying coastal areas to disappear underwater. Ice in the Arctic Ocean might also melt, but it wouldn't affect sea levels as much because it is already in the water.

Scientists think global warming might already be having an impact on life at the poles. There is much less sea ice around Antarctica than there used to be, and huge numbers of penguins have disappeared. In the eastern Canadian Arctic, caribou numbers have fallen drastically because there is more snow than there used to be. Elsewhere in the Arctic, however, caribou numbers have risen, perhaps because warmer summers have made their food more abundant.

Plants and animals in warmer parts of the world might be able to survive global warming by moving to cooler places as the world warms up. But the species at the poles simply have nowhere else to go.

The Ozone Holes

The sun gives life to almost everything on Earth, but sunlight also contains ultraviolet light, which is harmful to plants, animals, and people. Normally, an outer part of Earth's

 ## Could the World Drown?

Scientists are worried that global warming might raise sea levels by melting polar ice. The huge ice sheet that covers Lesser Antarctica already shows signs of collapsing. If it were to crumble into the ocean, sea levels around the world would rise by at least 17 feet (5 m). Low-lying towns, like Miami and New Orleans, would disappear underwater (right). Greenland's ice sheet is another cause for concern. If that melted, sea levels would go up 20 feet (6 m). And if the colossal Greater Antarctica ice sheet melted, sea levels would go up another 200 feet (61 m)—though scientists don't think that's likely to happen for a long time.

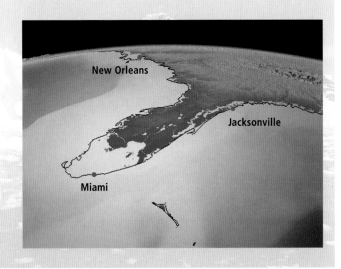

New Orleans

Jacksonville

Miami

Antarctic scientists use helium-filled weather balloons to study the ozone hole high over Antarctica. These researchers have adapted a balloon to photograph penguin colonies.

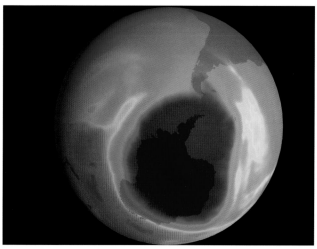

The deep blue area in this satellite picture is the ozone hole over Antarctica in winter 1998. The hole has since widened and now covers parts of South America, too.

 ## Disaster in Alaska

The environment paid a high price for arctic oil in 1989, when an oil tanker, the *Exxon Valdez*, ran into a rocky reef in Prince William Sound, Alaska, and its contents leaked into the sea. It wasn't the world's biggest oil spill, but it was one of the most dramatic—thousands of fish, seabirds, and otters perished in the resulting slick. The accident proved very expensive for the Exxon oil company. It had to pay about $1 billion to clean up the area, and the local fishermen sued the company for $5 billion for the economic damage it caused them.

atmosphere called the ozone layer screens out some of this dangerous light. The ozone works like a thin layer of sun cream spread over the whole Earth. But chemicals released into the atmosphere from such inventions as the aerosol can and refrigerator have eaten away at the ozone layer, and much more ultraviolet light can now get through.

Scientists found the first hole in the ozone layer over Antarctica in 1985, and another hole was discovered over the Arctic about a decade later. Almost every year since then, the ozone holes have grown in size. In 2000, scientists working for NASA found that the Antarctic ozone hole was three times bigger than the whole of the United States.

Off-road vehicles crush the slow-growing plants of the tundra, leaving scars that can take decades to heal.

Without the ozone layer, living things are much more at risk from ultraviolet radiation. For people, this means more chance of skin cancer and cataracts (a clouding of the eyes that can lead to blindness). Ultraviolet radiation slows down the growth of phytoplankton in the ocean and can even stop them growing altogther. It also damages the DNA of many animals, which can harm the way they grow and reproduce.

No one really knows what effects the ozone hole might have in the future, but the poles are likely to suffer the most. If there is less phytoplankton in the Antarctic, there will be fewer krill. And if there are fewer krill, there will be fewer fish, penguins, seals, and whales, and less food from the ocean for humans.

Oil and Gas

People have long seen the poles as a source of great wealth. In the 18th and 19th centuries, millions of furs were exported from the Arctic by ship to Britain and North America. More recently, Alaska and Siberia have produced vast amounts of oil and natural gas. This has meant the construction of oil rigs, oil-handling complexes, and some of the

biggest pipelines on Earth. The gleaming Trans-Alaska pipeline, for example, runs all the way from Prudhoe Bay on the north coast of Alaska to Valdez on the south coast. The oil industry has also brought new highways and towns to what used to be wilderness.

Many people see such changes as progress. The world needs oil, and it must come from somewhere. Oil has brought wealth to people of the Arctic, helping them build homes and schools. But not everyone agrees that a growing oil industry is a sign of progress. Highways, towns, and factories can damage the arctic wilderness, and oil slicks like the

Oil Versus Wildlife

In 2001, the United States government decided to allow oil companies to extract oil from a protected area of Alaskan tundra—the Arctic National Wildlife Refuge (below). Most of the Refuge is classified as protected wilderness, but the coastal plain in the north never had full wilderness status. If Congress approves the government's recommendation, new oil-drilling plants will appear on the north coast, taking the place of important breeding sites for polar bears and caribou. Environmental groups are determined to fight the plans, however.

one from the *Exxon Valdez* tanker in 1989 are a constant threat. As the world's need for oil increases, pressure grows to build oil wells in more remote places. Today, environmentalists are worried by plans to drill and extract oil from the Arctic National Wildlife Refuge in northeast Alaska. Although the world's nations have agreed not to take oil out of Antarctica for 50 years, there may come a time when they change their minds. No one knows what effect that would have on the world's last, untouched areas of wilderness.

A Brighter Future?

With huge threats like global warming and the ozone hole, the future looks uncertain for the wildlife of the arctic tundra and polar deserts. But things may not be as bad as they seem. The great auk became extinct in the Arctic because people once paid too little attention to the effect we have on the planet. Today, there is much greater awareness that Earth is a fragile planet and that we must all look after it. If people are wise enough to realize that the Arctic and Antarctica are among the greatest jewels of the natural world, these precious places will survive into the future. If not, we may lose them forever.

Caribou trudge past the Trans-Alaska pipeline. The pipeline delivers 17 percent of the United States's oil supply.

Glossary

Algonquian: A family of Native American languages spoken by people in eastern Canada and the eastern United States.

amphibian: A cold-blooded animal that spends part of its life in water and part on land, such as a frog, toad, or salamander.

amphipod: A shrimplike animal. Some amphipods live in the ocean in polar regions.

antarctic circle: An imaginary line drawn around the South Pole on which there is midnight sun for one day in midsummer.

arctic circle: An imaginary line drawn around the North Pole on which there is midnight sun for one day in midsummer.

arid: Having a dry climate. Deserts are arid.

atmosphere: The layer of air around Earth.

aurora: A colorful glow in the night sky near the poles.

biome: A major division of the living world, distinguished by its climate and wildlife. Tundra, desert, and temperate grasslands are examples of biomes.

blubber: A layer of fat under the skin of some water-living mammals such as seals, walruses, and whales.

carbon dioxide: A gas released when fuel burns. Carbon dioxide is one of the main gases causing global warming.

carnivore: A meat-eating animal.

climate: The pattern of weather that happens in one place during an average year.

cold-blooded: Having a body temperature that depends on the surroundings. Reptiles are cold-blooded, for example.

colony: A population of animals living in the same place, such as a group of nesting seabirds.

desert: A place that receives less than 10 inches (250 mm) of rainfall a year.

domestic animal: An animal kept by people, usually as a pet, farm animal, or pack animal.

dormant: So inactive as to appear lifeless. Plant seeds often lie dormant until the soil moistens.

ecosystem: A collection of living animals and plants that function together with their environment. Ecosystems include food chains.

equator: An imaginary line around Earth, midway between the North and South poles.

ermine: A type of white weasel that lives on the arctic tundra.

evaporate: To turn into a gas (vapor). Water becomes part of the air when it evaporates.

fertile: Able to sustain plant growth. Farmers try to make soil more fertile when growing crops.

food chain: Scientists can place animals and plants living in one place into a series that links each animal with the plant or animal that it eats. Plants are usually at the bottom of a food chain with large carnivores at the top.

glacier: A river of ice that flows slowly off a mountain or ice sheet.

global warming: The gradual warming of Earth's climate, thought to be caused in part by pollution of the atmosphere.

herbivore: A plant-eating animal.

hibernation: A period of dormancy that some animals go through during winter.

ice age: A period in history when Earth's climate was cooler. The last ice age ended about 10,000 years ago.

iceberg: A huge ice block floating in the sea, having broken from a glacier or ice sheet.

ice cap: A thick layer of ice covering land near the poles. The largest ice cap is on Antarctica.

insulate: To keep warm by trapping a layer of still air.

ivory: A white material that forms the tusks of walruses or elephants.

mammal: A warm-blooded animal that feeds its young on milk. Mice, bats, and whales are all mammals.

ozone: A gas that forms a layer in the upper atmosphere. The ozone layer shields Earth from some of the sun's ultraviolet radiation.

peninsula: A narrow strip of land surrounded on three sides by water.

permafrost: Permanently frozen ground under the surface of tundra and polar desert.

phytoplankton: Tiny, plantlike organisms that float in the surface waters of oceans and lakes.

polar desert: The main biome in Antarctica, northernmost Canada, and Greenland. Polar desert gets very little rain or snow, and the ground is usually barren or covered with snow and ice.

predator: An animal that eats other animals.

rain forest: A lush forest that gets lots of rain. Tropical rain forests grow in the tropics; temperate rain forests grow in cool places, such as the west coast of North America.

shrubland: A biome that mainly contains shrubs, such as the chaparral of California.

species: A particular type of organism. Cheetahs are a species, but birds are not, because there are many different types of birds.

taiga: A biome in the north of Canada, Europe, and Russia that mainly contains conifer trees.

temperate: Between the tropics and the cold, polar regions.

temperate forest: A biome of the temperate zone that mainly contains broadleaf trees.

temperate grassland: A biome of the temperate zone that mainly contains grassland.

tropical forest: Forest growing in Earth's tropical zone (near the equator), such as rain forest or monsoon forest.

tropical grassland: A biome of the tropical zone that mainly contains grassland. Tropical grassland dotted with trees is called savanna.

tundra: A biome of the far north, made up of treeless plains covered with small plants.

ultraviolet: Invisible rays from the sun that are similar to light. Plants use ultraviolet rays to make food.

warm-blooded: Having a constantly warm body temperature. Mammals and birds are warm-blooded.

water vapor: The gas that forms when water evaporates.

zooplankton: Tiny animals and animal-like organisms that live in the surface of oceans and lakes.

Further Research

Books

Allaby, Michael. *Polar Regions: Biomes of the World.* Danbury, CT: Grolier, 1999.
Fothergill, Alastair. *Life in the Freezer: A Natural History of the Antarctic.* London: BBC Books, 1993.
Lansing, Frank. *Shackleton's Incredible Voyage.* New York: Caroll & Graf, 1999.
Lynch, Wayne. *A is for Arctic: Natural Wonders of a Polar World.* Willowdale, Ont., Canada: Firefly Books, 1996.

Websites

Arctic Studies Center: http://www.mnh.si.edu/arctic/
(Information and exhibits about wildlife of the Arctic, its history, and its peoples.)
Wild Arctic Activities: http://www.seaworld.org/arctic/
(Lots of varied information and fun activities.)
Antarctica: The End of the Earth: http://www.pbs.org/wnet/nature/antarctica/index.html
(A great educational site with information, photos, and activities.)

Index

Page numbers in *italics* refer to picture captions.

Picture Credits

Key: l – left, r – right, m – middle, t – top, b – bottom. **Ardea**: Jean-Paul Ferrero 11, 34b, 42; Francois Gohier 16; Martin W. Grosnick 8; Edwin Mickleburgh 1, 46/47, 48b; S. Roberts 23; Graham Robertson 38, 58t; John E. Swedberg 57, 60b, 61; Andrey Zvoznikov 7l, 36t, 39b, 41b; **Bruce Coleman**: John Shaw 34t; Staffan Widstrand 22, 50, 52; **Corbis**: Gary Braasch 59b; Raymond Gehman 24; Wolfgang Kaehler 60t; Galen Rowell 53; Shepard Sherbell 18; Brian A. Vikander 6r, 27; **Greenland Guide**: www.greenland-guide.gl 48t; **Image Bank**: David W. Hamilton 30b, 45; Joseph Van Os 41m; **Lamont-Doherty Earth Observatory**: William Haxby 58b; **NASA**: Goddard Space Flight Center Scientific Visualization Studio 59t; **NHPA**: A.N.T. 11 (inset); B. and C. Alexander 17, 21t, 21b, 26, 29, 32, 44, 51, 54; G. I. Bernard 35; Hellio and Van Ingen 9; Paal Hermansen 7r, 55; Rich Kirchner 16, 46t; Stephen Krasemann 20; **Oxford Scientific Films**: Ben Osborne 25; Kim Westerskov 15; **PhotoDisc**: Geostock 40; Robert Glusic 4m; Bruce Heinemann 5l; Jack Hollingsworth 5m; Photolink 5r, 6m, 7m, 30/31, 33, 36b, 39t/l, 39t/r; Karl Weatherly 4r. **Front cover**: FLPA: Thomas Mangelsen/Minden Pictures **Front cover inserts**: Photolibrary.com: Schultz Jeff; NHPA: B. & C. Alexander; PhotoDisc.